Early China and the Wall

Peter Nancarrow

Published in cooperation with Cambridge University Press
Lerner Publications Company, Minneapolis

Editors' Note: In preparing this edition of *The Cambridge Topic Books* for publication, the editors have made only a few minor changes in the original material. In some isolated cases, British spelling and usage were altered in order to avoid possible confusion for our readers. Whenever necessary, information was added to clarify references to people, places, and events in British history. An index was also provided in each volume.

LIBRARY OF CONGRESS CATALOGING IN PUBLICATION DATA

Nancarrow, Peter, 1939-
  Early China and the Wall.

  (A Cambridge Topic Book)
  Includes index.
  SUMMARY: Traces the history of China from the earliest times to about 50 B.C. and discusses the origins of walled fortifications that eventually resulted in the building of the Great Wall.

  1. China—History—1766 B.C.-220 A.D.—Juvenile literature. 2. Wall of China—Juvenile literature. [1. China—History—1766 B.C.-200 A.D. 2. Wall of China] I. Title.

DS744.N36 1980   931   80-7446
ISBN 0-8225-1218-1

This edition first published 1980 by Lerner Publications Company
by permission of Cambridge University Press.

Original edition copyright © 1978 by Cambridge University Press
as part of *The Cambridge Introduction to the History of Mankind: Topic Book.*

International Standard Book Number: 0-8225-1218-1
Library of Congress Catalog Card Number: 80-7446

Manufactured in the United States of America.

This edition is available exclusively from:
Lerner Publications Company, 241 First Avenue North, Minneapolis, Minnesota 55401

2 3 4 5 6 7 8 9 10 85 84 83 82

Contents

Introduction *p.5*

1 The Chinese history of the Wall *p.7*
The earliest legends *p.8*
The earliest remains *p.9*
The first villages *p.10*
The earliest walls *p.10*

2 From pre-history to history *p.13*
The discovery of bronze *p.13*
Shang—the first historical regime *p.14*
The fortune-tellers *p.15*
A Shang city *p.15*
The bronze crafts of the Shang *p.18*
China-ware *p.20*
Poetry *p.20*
The fall of Shang *p.22*

3 The Chou dynasty *p.23*
The 'Chinese' way of life *p.26*
Confucius *p.27*
The impact of iron *p.28*

4 The Warring States *p.29*
Walls between the kingdoms *p.31*
Walls against the barbarians *p.31*
The rise of the kingdom of Ch'in *p.34*
The Lord Shang *p.35*

5 The Ch'in empire *p.38*
The Great Wall of China *p.39*
The collapse of the Ch'in empire *p.40*

6 The Han dynasty *p.44*
Expansion of the empire *p.44*
More wall-building *p.44*
The Han wall and the men who guarded it *p.46*

Guide to pronunciation of Chinese names *p.48*

Index p.49
Acknowledgments p.51

Modern China

Introduction

The picture on the next page shows part of the Great Wall of China, where it crosses the mountains near Peking. The map opposite shows how the remains of the Great Wall stretch right from the coast of China to the deserts of central Asia. If you study the picture carefully, you can see that the wall is built of bricks and stone; but what we can see today is only a few hundred years old. It was extensively repaired during the Ming dynasty (AD 1368 to AD 1644). We know that the origins of the Great Wall lie much further back in time, and we shall see how a Great Wall, over two thousand miles (three thousand kilometres) long, had already been built in China long before the Romans built Hadrian's Wall across the north of Britain. In this book we shall not only find out about the Wall, we shall also look at the people who lived in the area which corresponds to modern China, and discover how the people we call 'Chinese', and their country, came into being.

One of the obvious questions which we can ask about such an enormous landmark as the Great Wall of China is: why was it built? Why, in fact, should a wall be built across mountains and into the desert, when its very length was so great that even in less difficult country it would have needed enormous amounts of material and labour?

To answer this question we need to know when the Wall was built and what was happening at that time.

Going on from this question we can then ask how such an enormous wall was built. The sheer size of it is hard to imagine. A British surveyor, who saw the Wall in 1793, said that even to build its watch-towers would have taken as much brick and stone as the buildings of the whole of London in his day. Remember that even the repairs of the Ming period were done long before modern machinery was thought of.

Finally we might ask: who was it who thought of building the Great Wall in the first place?

below: *The Great Wall of China near Peking. The early walls were built across a landscape like this. The builders took advantage of the steep valleys to make it even more difficult for an enemy to attack. The buildings on the right are on the Chinese side of the wall.*

1 The Chinese history of the Wall

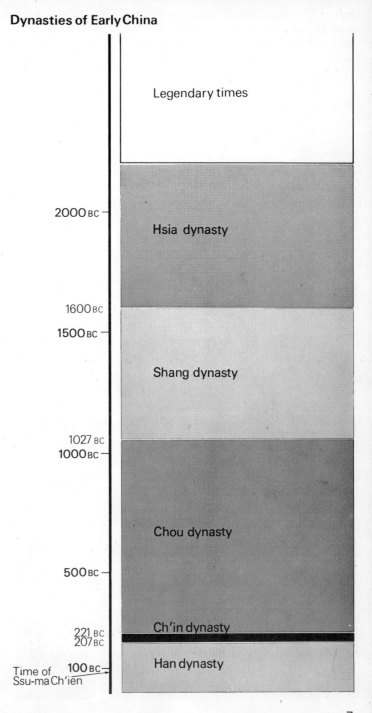

Dynasties of Early China

Legendary times

2000 BC

Hsia dynasty

1600 BC
1500 BC

Shang dynasty

1027 BC
1000 BC

Chou dynasty

500 BC

221 BC
207 BC

Ch'in dynasty

Time of Ssu-ma Ch'ien   100 BC

Han dynasty

The Chinese have been writing history books about their own country for over two thousand years. As many of these have survived until today, we are able to find definite answers to most of our questions about the Wall.

The oldest complete Chinese history book that we know about was written around 90 BC by Ssu-ma Ch'ien, Grand Historian of the Chinese Emperor's Court. His book was called the *Historical Annals*. It tells the whole history of China, as he had heard of it, from the earliest times up to the period of his own life, and it can still be read in much the same words that he wrote down. He thought that the territory controlled by the Chinese empire in his day had always been ruled over by kings and emperors in a system similar to that of the Han emperors who ruled during his lifetime. Chinese history is traditionally divided into *dynasties*, each of which consists of a succession of hereditary rulers. The chart shows the succession of dynasties which Ssu-ma Ch'ien wrote about, and the times at which they were thought to have existed. Now, let us see whether Ssu-ma Ch'ien can tell us anything about the Great Wall.

In Chapter 88 of the *Historical Annals*, we find the following paragraph:

'When the state of Ch'in had unified the empire, Meng T'ien was sent north with three hundred thousand men to chase off the barbarian tribes of Jung and Ti, and to control the land which lay to the south of the Yellow River. He was also told to build a long wall, following the lie of the land, in order to block off entry into the country. The wall stretched from Lint'ao to Liaotung, well over three thousand miles in all.'

Can you now work out the 'why, when and who' of the Great Wall as Ssu-ma Ch'ien saw it? You can find the 'why' and 'who' straight from Ssu-ma Ch'ien's description, and the chart will help you to work out the 'when'.

The answer to the question 'how' will have to wait until later

From earliest times China has suffered from floods and drought and the people have tried to control the rivers and improve cultivation. For centuries the valleys where the Yellow River flows through the Shensi mountains have been elaborately terraced to prevent erosion.

on, but even now it can be seen that Ssu-ma Ch'ien's words, in addition to answering three of our questions, have raised some new ones. Who were the people inside the Wall and who were the tribes of Jung and Ti? How were the two groups of people different, and why should they be kept apart? If we are to understand the answers to these questions we shall have to go right back to the beginnings of the people in the land which was to become China, and see how they developed.

The earliest legends

In China, just as in many other countries, myths and legends grew up to explain the origins of civilisation and the forces of Nature. The Chinese legends are about rulers and their ministers who were thought to have been responsible for creating the empire, and to have invented many of the basic techniques of everyday life, such as agriculture, silk production and the control of rivers. Many of the legends were included in early history books. Not only were the legendary kings and heroes thought of as people who had actually lived, but the legends even stated the times at which they lived, beginning with dates which work out around 3000 BC in our calendar. Even experts in interpreting early Chinese legends have had difficulty in working out the sequence of the legendary figures. If we are to get a clear picture of very early times, we have to try to find some other source of information.

below: Two of the tools used by Peking Man. The hammer-stone, about 3 in (8 cm) long, was used to strike and chip stones to make tools like the scraper (length 3·5 in, 8·5 cm). Scrapers would have been used to shape wood, to skin and dismember animals and to scrape the skins clean.

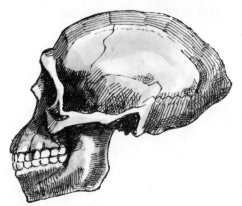

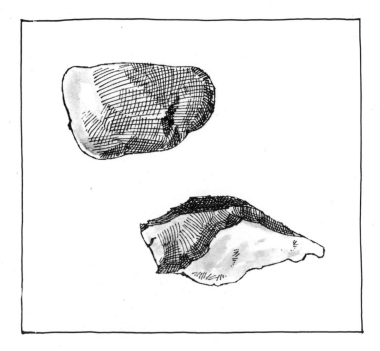

In 1929 part of a fossil skull, about 500,000 years old, was found by archaeologists excavating near Peking. This confirmed the belief in Peking Man whose existence had been deduced from a single tooth found at the beginning of the century.

The first two drawings show the tooth, and the skull that was put together from the fragments found. Archaeologists could then make a model of the head of Peking Man. The third drawing shows what they think Peking Man looked like.

The earliest remains

The oldest evidence of human occupation in China is in the form of archaeological remains, including the famous fossil bones of Peking Man, about half a million years old. Although other more ancient remains have been discovered, this takes us back long before Ssu-ma Ch'ien's earliest legends. Judging by the stone tools, animal bones, charcoal, charred stones and nuts which were found with the fossils, this remote cave-dweller of China could make and use both fire and tools. He was a hunter who caught animals for food and cooked their flesh. To survive all the year round, Peking Man must have followed the animals he hunted, and so he would not have lived always in the same place.

below: Archaeologists excavating a rectangular building at Panp'o village, which was occupied from about 4000 BC. This large house had storage spaces and ovens. Excavators found pottery, and stone and bone tools.

Many possessions of the earliest villagers have been found at Panp'o. Here are some examples:
  A polished stone chisel 3 in (8 cm) long.
  A bone arrow or harpoon head 2·5 in (6 cm) long. It seems likely that the village was sited near the banks of a stream which would supply fish for food and water for crops. The 'harpoon' may well have been used for attacking fish.

  A bone needle, 6·5 in (16·5 cm) long; needles of all sizes down to about an inch have been found at the village, indicating that the thread and the needlework were comparatively fine.

The first villages

There were legends about a Spirit Farmer. Even so we do not know exactly when Man first began to cultivate plants and raise animals, but once this had happened it changed his way of life. He could begin to live all the year round in the same place. He could grow the plants and keep the animals where he wanted them. He would not have to move about as the seasons changed but could stay in his own village. The existence of the early legend of the farmer does however show the great importance which was given to agriculture, with its more settled way of life. One of the best examples of an early village is at Panp'o in Shensi province. Archaeologists have excavated this site and the remains have been preserved as a museum.

The earliest walls

With the civilisation of village life came conflict. The village settlements may have become the target of attack from neighbouring villages. They may have been raided by hunting

A bowl and jar made of red pottery. The jar has a characteristic pattern of rope marks. With a cord threaded through the handles the jar could be lowered into the stream and filled with water. The bowl stands 7·5 in (19 cm) high; the jar 17 in (43 cm).

tribes which had survived into the generally more settled Neolithic (New Stone Age) period in which the early villages were established. We cannot tell. However, the fact that many sites have defensive walls is a clear sign that the security of the villages was threatened from some direction.

It is unlikely that the threat came from wild animals, since the walls are far more massive than would have been needed to keep animals at bay. At one site, a perimeter wall was found in the form of a rectangular enclosure about 400 yards by 450 yards (350 m by 400 m). The excavations showed that when first built, this wall was about twenty feet (six metres) high and twenty-seven feet (eight metres) wide at its top. It seems that such a barrier must have been designed to withstand a joint attack by a determined enemy.

These Neolithic village defences are the earliest examples of wall-building which are known in this area. They are the first clues in the search for the origins of the Great Wall of China. We shall look at one of these village walls more closely to see if it can tell us how walls of this type were built.

The first noticeable thing about the wall is that it is made up

Pounded earth walling under construction. Notice the similarities between the modern photograph and the picture below, of Chinese wall builders, made in the third century AD.

of sharply defined layers of earth, each about five inches (thirteen centimetres) thick. Secondly, the top surface of the uppermost layer can be seen to be covered all over with shallow dents, all roughly the same shape, as if they were all made by the same object. Finally, we can guess how hard the layers must be, since they have lasted for five thousand years without crumbling away completely. How do you think these hard layers of earth were built up? Although we do not have any direct evidence, walls like this continued to be built throughout Chinese history. There are many pictures in Chinese books showing how earth was beaten down with rammers into an open wooden frame until it formed an extremely hard layer. After this the frame was raised, re-filled with earth, the next layer rammed down, and so on until the wall reached the required height. The photograph shows a wall being built in exactly this way in recent times.

2 From pre-history to history

The discovery of bronze

Archaeological evidence shows that village life continued for many centuries without great change, right up to the period in which Ssu-ma Ch'ien placed the Hsia dynasty, while skills in pottery, stone-working and tool-making improved steadily. Evidence from burial sites shows that social customs and religious beliefs were also developing gradually. However, this pattern of village life changed about 1600 BC. One cause of this was almost certainly the growth of new skills in making bronze. Bronze is a mixture, or alloy, mainly of copper and tin. It was made by heating minerals which naturally contained those metals. Although the earliest examples of bronze objects date

The twin-moulding method of casting bronze

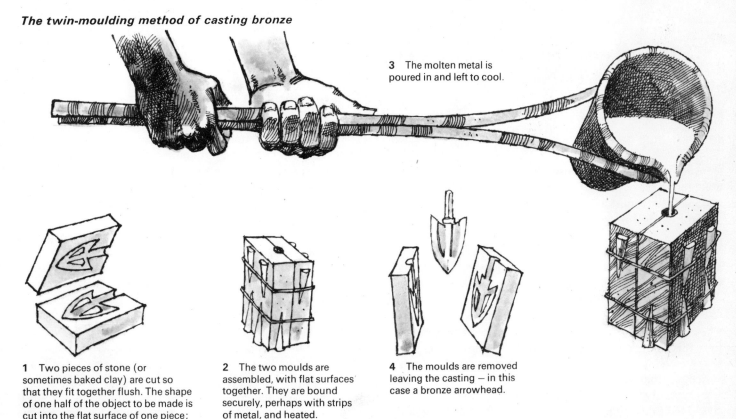

3 The molten metal is poured in and left to cool.

1 Two pieces of stone (or sometimes baked clay) are cut so that they fit together flush. The shape of one half of the object to be made is cut into the flat surface of one piece; the shape of the other half of the object, which may or may not be the same, is cut into the flat surface of the second mould.

2 The two moulds are assembled, with flat surfaces together. They are bound securely, perhaps with strips of metal, and heated.

4 The moulds are removed leaving the casting — in this case a bronze arrowhead.

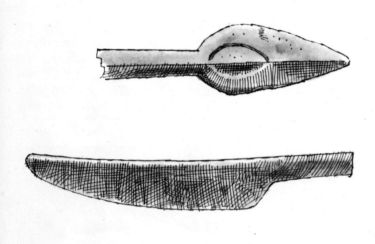

Although no bronze weapons have survived from this very early period, the pictures on this page show some of the earliest bronze weapons which *are* known, and which are no doubt similar to what would have been made earlier.

The increasing use of bronze which began at this time marked the beginning of the Shang dynasty. If you look again at the chart on page 7, you will see that Ssu-ma Ch'ien places the Shang immediately after the Hsia dynasty, but as we shall see, there is a great difference between what we know about the Hsia and what we know about the Shang.

Shang—the first historical regime

We have already seen that a lot is known about the early village dwellers, but no written records have survived, in spite of the discovery of some fragments of pottery with a primitive form of writing on them. Because of this, the Hsia dynasty and its predecessors must remain as legends.

The Shang period brings us from pre-history firmly into history. This is because Shang written records have survived for three thousand years and more until the present day. Many of the details in Ssu-ma Ch'ien's book have been confirmed by checking them against records from the Shang dynasty itself. These records were not written on paper, but were inscribed on bones, and many thousands of whole and broken bones, with written inscriptions, have been discovered by archaeologists. The bones form a valuable source of information, since the writing on them is an early version of Chinese script, and much of it can be understood today. For example, one set of bone inscriptions contains a list of the Shang kings, probably used in the worship of the spirits of dead royal ancestors. This list largely confirms the list of Shang kings given by Ssu-ma Ch'ien. At this point, then, we can begin to place stronger reliance on Ssu-ma Ch'ien's account, particularly when it is confirmed by archaeological discoveries.

from about this period, because of the high degree of skill which was used to make them, it has been estimated that the craft of making bronze must have been developing for about a century previously. So bronze would have been known as early as 1700 BC.

Some of the oldest bronze objects known are knives and arrowheads. It is thought that the improvements which these weapons represent, compared with the clumsier stone and bone weapons of Neolithic times, gave a distinct advantage in warfare to those who could make them. No doubt the skilled craftsmen who could provide these weapons formed a valuable group. It is from this point that a new pattern of civilisation emerges. There is now a highly specialised craft, which is not directly related to agriculture, but which forms an important part of the activity of a community. We speak of the period when this trend developed as the Bronze Age. We see that the centre of power changed from the small village communities of Neolithic times to the larger settlements, or towns, where farmers and craftsmen lived together.

A Shang dynasty jade ring. The diameter is about 6 in . As well as being used in religious ceremonies, the ring o have been used to measure the movements of the stars ment with the serrations around the edge.

chariots were like, how the horses were harnessed, and what weapons the charioteer carried. As well as swords and spears, the Shang developed a weapon known as a *ko*, which looked rather like a dagger blade fastened to project sideways from a long wooden handle. Many of these have been discovered. They were clearly a common weapon in armies of the Shang period. Jade versions of many of the bronze weapons have also been found. It would appear that these were mainly for show, not for fighting.

The bronze crafts of the Shang

The surprising thing about Shang bronze technology is that nearly all the articles which we know about are of the highest standard. Yet there is very little evidence of a slow development leading up to this level. Once Shang bronzecasting had reached this standard, it continued for many centuries. It produced a rich variety of vessels of different shapes and ornamentation for use in religious sacrifices to the ancestors and the gods. If you look closely at the pictures on these pages, you will see that not only were complicated shapes produced, but also the decorative patterns are very sharply defined.

How were these vessels made? Starting from the use of baked clay moulds (see page 13), fragments of which have been found, even complex shapes like the three-legged vessel opposite could be made. A number of separate mould parts had to be fastened together, but, by arranging the patterns carefully, the Shang bronzesmiths could conceal the joints.

Another method which was probably used, but for which we have no direct evidence, started with a wax model which was carefully coated with clay. When the clay was baked to harden it, the wax would melt and run out, leaving a hollow space in the fired clay block which could be filled up with molten bronze which solidified to form a metal replica of the original wax

The fortune-tellers

The inscribed bones contain a lot of other information from Shang times. Many of the bones were used in fortune-telling, and are called 'oracle bones'. On important occasions, tortoise-shell was used instead of bone. When the fortune-teller was asked a question, he wrote it on a bone, and then placed a heated bronze point on the bone to make it crack. The answer to the question depended on the pattern of cracks in the bone. The inscription was cut into the bone to make it more permanent, and the bone was then stored away. It is clear from the bones that sacrifices were not only made to the spirits of the ancestors of the Shang kings, but also to a number of gods of whom the most powerful was Shang-ti, 'the Ruler Above'.

From the system of dating in the oracle bone inscriptions we can tell that the Shang people had an advanced calendar. This has been confirmed by the discovery of a bone inscribed with the calendar of the first two months of the year corresponding to 1272 BC. Astronomy was also well developed, and records of five eclipses of the moon have been found, which, by scientific calculation, can be shown to have occurred in 1373, 1344, 1311, 1282 and 1279 BC.

The oracle bone inscriptions also include the names of the fortune-tellers, and it appears that there was a regular group of people involved in this work. These men with their skill in writing, and their task of official fortune-telling and record-keeping, seem to have formed something like a Civil Service for the Shang court.

A Shang city

In his story of the beginning of the Shang dynasty, Ssu-ma Ch'ien tells us that Duke T'ang, a strong local ruler in the west, gathered an army together and attacked King Chieh of the Hsia dynasty. Duke T'ang won the campaign, and took the title of King of Shang.

left: *A model of the tomb of a Shang king showing the central grave pit, about 30 feet (9 m) square, the ramps down which the funeral procession passed, and the skeletons of the slaves.*

opposite: *Ritual dances are performed in the walled Shang city before the army sets out. This picture by a modern artist shows what chariots and musical instruments may have looked like.*

increased also. Craftsmen had found it easier and safer to live in bigger communities, where they could hold markets and defend themselves. So cities arose, each with its own government which ruled and protected the city itself and the surrounding villages that supplied the city with food. The Kingdom of Shang was only one of these, although the most powerful. Any of the other states which tried to challenge the Shang state were suppressed by military raids. To defend themselves against attack, the city-states continued the tradition begun by the earlier villages, and again built walls of beaten earth. These were now very large indeed, some being fifty feet (fifteen metres) thick and twenty-five feet (eight metres) high.

The Shang rulers used a series of different sites for their capital city during the period. The biggest and last of these was the great city of Yin, near present-day Anyang. The site has been extensively investigated, and we can tell in some detail what life in the Shang period must have been like. Buildings as well as walls were similar to those of the villages, although much larger, and a royal palace area has been found. Again, pottery was in general use as in the pre-Shang period, but new designs and types were developed. Another feature which continued and developed in the Shang period was the carving of jade, but the most interesting aspects of the Shang are those which appear for the first time, and we shall now look at some of these.

Much valuable information about the Shang has come from tombs, since the Shang continued the customs of their predecessors in burying goods to accompany the dead to their after-life. Some of the most impressive examples of Shang art and ornaments have come from the royal tombs at Anyang. The size of the tombs can be seen from the picture and the magnificence of the burial is clear from what was excavated. The Shang king was accompanied in death by precious articles, weapons, chariots, teams of horses, and human sacrifices so that he would have plentiful equipment and servants in the after-life. From the remains in the tombs we can tell what Shang

Ssu-ma Ch'ien's history implies that the Shang kings ruled over a large area, but the real situation appears to have been rather different. Archaeological remains show us that a number of cities had grown up by this time. Probably this had happened because crafts had increased – metalwork, woodwork, cloth-making and pottery, for example – and trade and wealth had

Shang bronzes. Three bronze vessels used by the Shang people in ceremonies. The one on the left is for wine. It is 22 in (55 cm) high. The middle one, also for wine, is made in the shape of a two-headed animal. It is 17 in (43 cm) high. The third is a food vessel 9 in (23 cm) high.

The bronze knife with a decorated handle was probably made by the lost-wax method. It is 10 in (25 cm) long.

model. The use of this method would explain how some intricate bronze articles, which could not have been made by ordinary moulds, were produced.

It is clear from archaeological investigations that the bronzesmiths occupied a separate part of the city. Like the fortune-tellers, they probably formed a privileged group in Shang life, receiving special rewards in return for their special skill in making the bronze articles needed by the Shang court.

19

A yellow glazed pottery vase from the Shang dynasty. This is an example of the earliest known pottery ware covered with a high fired glaze. Below the shoulder it has been made by the traditional method of beating clay against a stone mould with a rope-covered paddle; the rim has been completed on a wheel. Height 11 in (28 cm).

smooth finish to a hand-made vessel and also to fashion vessels from the raw clay. Thus by the end of the Shang dynasty, advanced skills had been reached in the manufacture of pottery. It is no accident that the people who were able to develop high-temperature kilns for pottery were also able to smelt bronze.

Poetry

As well as working as scribes (see page 15) the Shang fortune-tellers took part in the royal sacrifices to the ancestors and gods of the rulers. They offered grain, wine and animals in ritual ceremonies. The offerings would be placed in the various bronze vessels, a special vessel for each one. Dancing, music and poetry accompanied these sacrifices. One of the ancient collections of poetry, made before the time of Ssu-ma Ch'ien, includes poems which refer to the Shang dynasty, and which were probably handed down from that period. Here is part of one of these poems:

> Heaven bade the dark bird
> To come down and bear the Shang,
> Who dwelt in the lands of Yin so wide.
> Of old God bade the warlike T'ang
> To partition the frontier lands.
> To those lands was he assigned as their lord;
> Into his keeping came all realms.
> The early lords of Shang
> Received a charge that was never in peril.
> In the time of Wu Ting's grandsons and sons,
> Wu Ting's grandsons and sons,
> Warlike kings ever conquered,
> With dragon-banners and escort of ten chariots.

China-ware

Have you ever wondered why we call some kinds of pottery 'china'? The reason is that when European merchants eventually found their way to China in the Middle Ages, they found that the Chinese could make a very fine white pottery, so thin that you could see a light shining through it. This pottery was porcelain, and it became known in the West as 'China-ware'.

Porcelain is made by coating a fine white clay with a material known as a glaze, and baking it at an extremely high temperature until the glaze merges into the clay. Even after seeing China-ware, it took European potters a long time to master the art. The skills of the Chinese potter came from the Shang period. The examples of village earthenware on page 10 were all hand made, and any decoration was on the surface. The Shang vessel shown on this page is covered in a glossy layer of glaze. From the hardness of the clay we can tell that it was fired at a much higher temperature than the earlier pottery.

Another skill which the Shang potters perfected was the use of the potter's wheel. The wheel enabled a potter to give a

Here are the same lines in Chinese. The characters are arranged in vertical columns reading from top to bottom and from right to left. In the poem, Yin is a name for the land of Shang, and Wu Ting was one of the descendants of T'ang, of whom we have already read on page 15.

龍　武　武　在　受　商　奄　方　正　古　宅　降　天
旂　王　丁　武　命　之　有　命　域　帝　殷　而　命
十　靡　孫　丁　不　先　九　厥　彼　命　土　生　玄
乘　不　子　孫　殆　后　有　后　四　彼　芒　商　鳥
　　勝　　　子　　　　　　　　　　　　武　四　芒
　　　　　　　　　　　　　　　　　　　方　湯　芒

Chinese writing

Chinese writing began as picture writing cut into bone or bronze. Then, from about 300 BC, Chinese was written with a brush on bamboo strips or on silk. The poem above is written with a modern pen which is usual nowadays.

The diagram opposite shows how one of the characters in the poem may have developed.

孫 This is the character sun, meaning grandson.

It is made up of two parts:

The left part 孑 means 'son' (possibly, from a 'stick-man' drawing of a woman carrying a child on her back).

Part of the character on the right, 系 (without the top stroke) used to mean 'silk' or 'something to bind with'.

The whole of the character on the right (called xí) means, among other things, 'connection' or 'relationship'.

Both together mean grandson.

Chime stones were among the oldest musical instruments in China. A clear ringing tone was produced by striking the stones suspended from a frame. This chime stone, decorated with a tiger-like figure, comes from a royal tomb at Anyang (see page 16). The picture on page 17 shows chime stones being played. Chinese musicians also played on bells, pipes and drums.

The fall of Shang

What picture can we now make of the Shang rulers? Clearly they were very wealthy, having a richly furnished court set in a large city. Also they must have been very powerful, judging from the military forces which they controlled and the way in which vast numbers of men could be slaughtered to accompany a dead ruler to his grave. Why, then, did the Shang dynasty fall?

Ssu-ma Ch'ien tells us that the final years of the dynasty were marked by a number of weak, degenerate rulers, the last of whom spent much of his time and wealth in holding drunken orgies. Eventually the time came when one of the rivals to Shang power, called the Chou people, moved from the west against the Shang and overthrew them. This took place in 1027 BC. The fall of Shang is spoken of in an ancient Chinese book, known as the *Book of Documents*, which although not written until later, records much of the early Chou period. From this book, on which Ssu-ma Ch'ien would have relied for some of his information, we can see the attitude taken by the Chou to the people they had conquered. After telling the assembled armies of Chou of the evils of the rule of King Shou of Shang, King Wu of Chou said: 'The crimes of Shang are all-pervasive; Heaven commands that Shang be destroyed. If I were not to obey Heaven, my own crime would be just as bad.'

3 The Chou dynasty

If you look back at Ssu-ma Ch'ien's list of dynasties on page 7, you will see that the Chou dynasty stretches right up to 221 BC, but the picture of a single Chou dynasty ruling from 1027 to 221 BC would be totally misleading. The first Chou rulers established control over a considerable part of China, but they had no means by which they personally could govern such a large area. For this reason they appointed noblemen from among their followers to govern the various districts of the country. The idea was that the noblemen should be loyal to the Chou ruling house, and govern their areas on behalf of the Chou rulers. This system worked quite well at first. The Chou dynasty exercised its rule through about forty small fiefs, as we call the lands of the noblemen, many of whom were relations of the Chou king. We can tell from ceremonial bronze vessels about the way in which the Chou rulers granted land to their noblemen. The grant was made with great ceremony, and when the vessel was made, it was inscribed with an account of the grant in the same sort of Chinese characters which the Shang had developed. Here is a picture of one of these bronze vessels:

A bronze vessel (length 14 in, 36 cm) which held water for ceremonial hand washing. The decoration of stylised birds is a feature of the Chou period. It is inscribed: 'In the king's first month, first quarter day, Kong-wu Hsiung of Ch'u ordered the casting of this yi. For a myriad of years may sons and grandsons perpetually use it for sacrifice.'

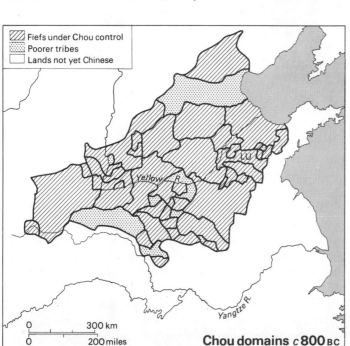

Fiefs under Chou control
Poorer tribes
Lands not yet Chinese

LU

Yellow R.

Yangtze R.

0   300 km
0   200 miles

Chou domains c 800 BC

Three typical shapes of bronze vessels. These were made by the Shang people. Those on the opposite page were made by the Chou. The water pots are 9 in (23 cm) high. The other vessels are in the same scale. Pots, buckets and vases were made in these shapes for many centuries.

Water pot

Wine bucket

Beaker or vase

The Chou people, then, saw their task as saving the people of Shang from their wicked rulers. The justification which the Chou are said in the *Book of Documents* to have given for this liberation was based on the argument that a ruler could only keep control of his land if he ruled it in accordance with the will of Heaven. If he failed to rule well, then Heaven would withdraw its support, and eventually a successor would rise and, with Heaven's approval, gain control. The new ruler in his turn had to govern in accordance with the will of Heaven, or he also would be deposed. Consequently neither the people, nor their new rulers, should feel that a conquest had taken place; the country was simply continuing under a rule which had been authorised by Heaven itself.

This continuity can clearly be seen in the case of the early Chou rulers. They viewed themselves as successors of the Shang, and although the customs of the Chou people had

originally been different from those of the Shang, the Chou absorbed the Shang way of life. You can see something of this from the bronze articles here. Weapons, pottery and written inscriptions were also similar under both dynasties. In fact, daily life under the early Chou was probably not a great deal different from that of the late Shang.

The system of fiefs soon became an ideal for Chinese government, but in practice the situation was never as neat and tidy as the map implies. At the beginning of the Chou dynasty the lands allotted to the noblemen were not all under their strict control since some did not have large enough fighting forces. In any case there were gaps between fiefs, generally the poorer lands, where less advanced tribes lived. Because of this, the pattern of control was constantly shifting. Alliances were made by the noblemen between themselves, and sometimes with the less advanced tribes whom they called 'barbarians'. As the

Water pot

Wine bucket

Beaker or vase

boundaries of the fiefs shifted and spread, squeezing out the barbarians, the more advanced way of life of the Chou spread over the whole area.

The struggle for power continued, and the Chou kings began to lose control of the situation. Finally in 771 BC the king was killed in an attack by one of the noblemen's armies on the Royal Domain of Chou. The Chou court fled to the east, but although they set up a new Chou kingdom, they no longer held any real authority over the area which they had previously controlled. Once this had happened, there was a more or less continuous struggle for power between the individual noblemen, and the boundaries between the different states changed even more rapidly.

Although the Chou kings had lost their political power as controllers of the other states, the years following 771 BC are still referred to as part of the Chou period, because the Chou king continued to be the religious head of the states. The first concern of the individual noblemen, however, was to consolidate their own political power. Stronger rulers would enter into alliances with weaker ones, and in time the stronger took over the weaker. Even so, military campaigns played a much less important part in the relationship between the states than might be expected, for, during the Chou period, not only was government carried out in accordance with a complicated ritual known as *The Rites*, but military campaigns were also undertaken according to prescribed regulations. Battles were more like organised tournaments, with a ban on the use of excessive force.

This period, from 771 BC to about 480 BC, is known as the *Spring and Autumn* period. This name comes from the title of a contemporary historical chronicle of the State of Lu, called *The Spring and Autumn Annals*.

right: *An artist's impression, from a much later time, which tries to show the building of the walls of the Chou capital city. There is a core of pounded earth, but the artist has anticipated later development by putting in a stone base and brick facings. The book from which this picture was taken describes the work as being done by the defeated Shang people.*

below: *This is an idealised plan of the way in which an early Chinese royal city would have been laid out. You can see three gateways in each wall with watchtowers above, the palace area in the centre and the network of broad roads.*

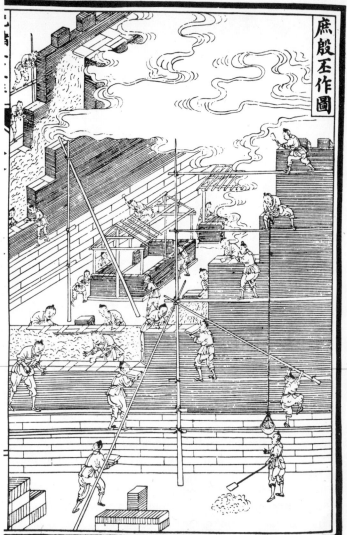

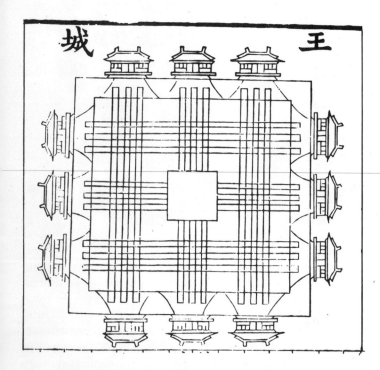

The 'Chinese' way of life

By the time of the Spring and Autumn period, the way of life which had existed under the Shang had changed greatly. Nevertheless certain things lasted long enough to become more and more a recognisable 'Chinese' way. Here are some examples:

The bigger towns, or cities, of the states were constructed on a four-square plan, with the royal palace facing south, and were defended by a perimeter wall.

The rest of the countryside was still largely agricultural, with people living in settled communities in villages or towns.

Bronze-casting and the making of pottery were still practised, and many of the older shapes of vessels were being made.

Ancestor-worship continued in a way which had originated even before the Shang.

26

right: *Confucius (551–479 BC).*

far right: *Mencius (c 372–289 BC). Both these drawings were made much later in the traditional way of showing these famous men.*

The system of writing which the Shang developed was still in use. This leads us to think that the language of the Chou period was very much like that of the Shang.

However, the Spring and Autumn period brought new facets to this 'Chinese' pattern, at least two of which are linked to the increasing warfare which was shortly to develop between the states.

Firstly, iron came into use in around 500 BC, and this led to an improvement in metal weapons as well as in other tools. Once again, the owners of more efficient weapons were at an advantage, and warfare spread just as it had when bronze weapons were perfected a thousand or so years earlier.

Secondly, there were men who hoped to use their minds to think up systems of government which would overcome the need for warfare, and bring back peace to the population. The most famous of these men was Confucius.

Confucius

Although Confucius was one of the most famous Chinese philosophers, very little is known about his life, and he himself left no written works. We learn most about the man and his thought from a collection of his sayings written down by the disciples of Confucius' own pupils.

As far as we know, Confucius was born in 551 BC. As a young man he received the education of a minor nobleman. Educated people of this time would normally seek employment in the high official posts in the courts of the various states, but it seems that Confucius never rose above the lowest appointments. However, he began to explain his theories to a group of pupils. It is this teaching which has been handed down to us.

The central point in the thought of Confucius is that mankind is of two sorts. The first of these is the *superior man*, who shows righteousness and humanity in his behaviour. The second is the *petty man* who lacks these qualities. It was the superior man, in Confucius' view, who should govern the petty man, and so his political philosophy is one of moral government, according to which the ruler 'governs' his people through his own example. According to Confucius, the early years of the Chou dynasty had been a golden age of moral government. It was his aim to restore this model. However, his high ideals never appealed to any of the rulers to whom he explained them. After travelling around the various states he returned to Lu, where he died in 479 BC.

The best-known follower of Confucius was Mencius, who lived from about 372 BC to 289 BC. As in the case of Confucius, most of our knowledge about Mencius' thought comes from the book which is known by his name, although it was actually

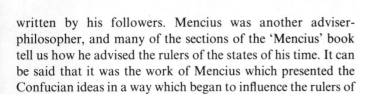

written by his followers. Mencius was another adviser-philosopher, and many of the sections of the 'Mencius' book tell us how he advised the rulers of the states of his time. It can be said that it was the work of Mencius which presented the Confucian ideas in a way which began to influence the rulers of the various states.

Mencius was the first follower of Confucius whom we know to have stated explicitly that human nature is basically good. According to Mencius, this accounts for the origin of *benevolence*, one of the principles praised by Confucius.

Not all Confucian philosophers were to agree with this view. Hsün-tzu, who lived from 298 BC to 238 BC argued that human nature was bad. He felt that men needed to be educated to develop goodness, and although Hsün-tzu was generally in agreement with Confucius, this view later developed to contribute to a rival school of philosophy known as Legalism.

The impact of iron

As we have seen, iron came into use among the Chinese around 500 BC. The first thing to be noted is that most iron objects were made from *cast* iron. This is different from the rest of the world, where cast iron was not produced until nearly two thousand years later. Casting of iron is quite a quick process. It now became possible to make large numbers of tools and weapons, and these spread fairly quickly into general use.

As in the case of bronze (see page 20), there is a connection between metal-working and pottery. Pottery kilns had been improving over the centuries, and they now gave the iron-founders the means to produce the very high temperatures which are needed to smelt iron and make it flow easily into moulds. At about the same time, efficient bellows had been

designed that enabled the heat of a kiln to be increased still further.

Clay was often used to make the moulds for casting iron, but some moulds for making iron were themselves made of iron. You can guess how skilled the iron-founder would have to be in controlling the temperature of the molten iron to avoid melting the mould in the process!

Not only was cast iron cheaper and more plentiful than bronze, but it was stronger and held a good cutting edge for a longer time. It was these qualities which made the iron weapons better than bronze ones. Armed with these new weapons, the states fought with each other more often and more bitterly, so that the years from 480 BC to 221 BC were known as the *Period of the Warring States*. The old rules of battle no longer applied. A militarily strong state was now able to occupy much larger areas of territory than before.

To defend this territory, the Warring States began to build defensive walls not only around their cities, but also along their frontiers. This marked a new departure in wall-building.

4 The Warring States

The Warring States

By now the way of life which we have called 'Chinese' had spread over the greater part of the area shown in this map. Now also the various 'Chinese' states began to struggle with each other to increase their control. The period of the Warring States was a time of so many changes that it would need dozens of maps to show exactly what happened. Instead, we shall use the map on this page, which shows the boundaries of the most important states in about 490 BC, and the chart below to show how the fortunes of these states changed as they struggled together. The map also shows where the most important of the early walls defending territories were built.

The Warring States

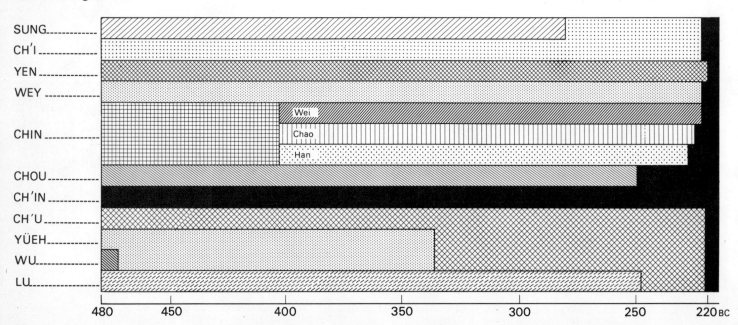

below: *Head of a life-size statue of one of the people of the state of Ch'in.*

Walls between the kingdoms

One of the earliest walls was built by the kingdom of Ch'i in north-east China in about 450 BC. It followed the line of the southern foothills of the T'ai Shan range of mountains, which had marked state boundaries in the past. Now this line was made more permanent and so the kingdom of Ch'i was easier to defend against attempts by the state of Lu to expand northwards. Certainly, the Lu never crossed the Ch'i wall.

The other walls on the map were not built for about another hundred years, and by this time the situation shown on the map had changed. The starting point in this change can, however, be seen before 550 BC in the increasing power of the kingdom of Ch'in (shown in the west of China on the map), and the subsequent breaking up of the kingdom of Chin (shown on the chart).

Chin was a kingdom which had covered a large area in northern China, but as it expanded further and further northwards into areas which had been occupied by barbarians, Chin became unstable and in 404 BC broke up into the three new kingdoms of Chao, Wei and Han.

In about 353 BC the new kingdom of Wei built a wall to protect itself against the expanding kingdom of Ch'in, which was pushing eastwards into the rest of China, but the strength of Ch'in was so great that it conquered Wei in spite of the wall. The kingdom of Wei survived in a much smaller area, far to the east, and built another wall soon after 350 BC to protect itself once again.

While Ch'in was expanding in the west of China, the kingdom of Ch'u in the south was also increasing in power, and in about 300 BC set up a line of fortifications across the road south from the kingdom of Han.

Walls against the barbarians

The stage of building walls inside China to mark the limits between the Chinese kingdoms was quickly followed by the building of a series of walls along the northern limits of China to mark and defend the boundary between China and the 'northern barbarians'. These were nomadic tribes not following the 'Chinese' way of life. Most of this stage of building took place within the space of twenty years or so. In about 306 BC the kingdom of Chao conquered the barbarians to the far north-west, with the hope of being able to attack Ch'in from this new area. This did not succeed, but in the same year Chao built a wall along its northern boundary to defend the area against re-occupation by the barbarians. Shortly after this, in 300 BC, the kingdom of Ch'in built a wall along the edge of its territory, linking up with the earlier wall built by the kingdom of Wei, and finally, in about 290 BC, the kingdom of Yen built a wall stretching from near the eastern end of the Chao wall almost to the coast.

Why did the pattern of wall-building change from the construction of 'inner' walls between the Chinese kingdoms to the construction of 'outer' walls between the Chinese and the peoples beyond China? Look at this map and you will see.

Apart from the areas south of the Yangtse river (which had not yet been penetrated by the Chinese to any extent), the land easy to cultivate lay well inside the 'outer' walls. These ran roughly along the edge of the land which it was possible to use for the agricultural way of life of the Chinese. Originally the Chinese kingdoms had expanded against each other and built the inner walls. After this, any further expansion had to take place outwardly. But this expansion could really only extend over areas suited to the Chinese way of life. Any Chinese going beyond these areas would have to follow the barbarian way of life. They would then have become identified with barbarians like the Jung and Ti tribes. So, just as the Chinese kingdoms had marked their internal boundaries by walls, they went on to mark their external boundaries in the same way. They built a line of defence which was to form the pattern of the northern frontier of China for nearly two thousand years.

How were these frontier walls built? At present we do not have any direct evidence to give us the answer, but city walls from the same period have been examined. These, like the earlier village and city walls, are made from layers of pounded earth. We can deduce from this that the longer territorial defence walls of the Warring States period were almost certainly built in the same way. At about this time also, more sophisticated methods of wall-building came into use; baked clay bricks were used as a facing to give protection to some walls. Also, in some cases, layers of reeds were placed in the wall as it was built to give added strength.

If these were the methods, who organised the building and where did the workers come from? These walls were hundreds of miles long. Tens of thousands of men must have been involved in building them. Imagine the planning behind such an operation, and the power of a ruler who could summon such vast numbers to work for him in this way.

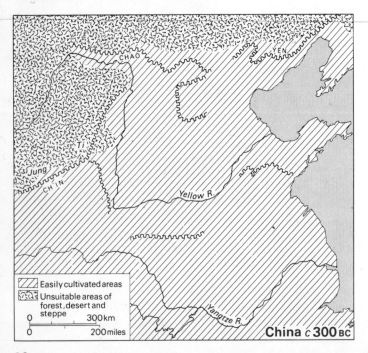

Easily cultivated areas
Unsuitable areas of forest, desert and steppe

0   300 km
0   200 miles

China c **300** BC

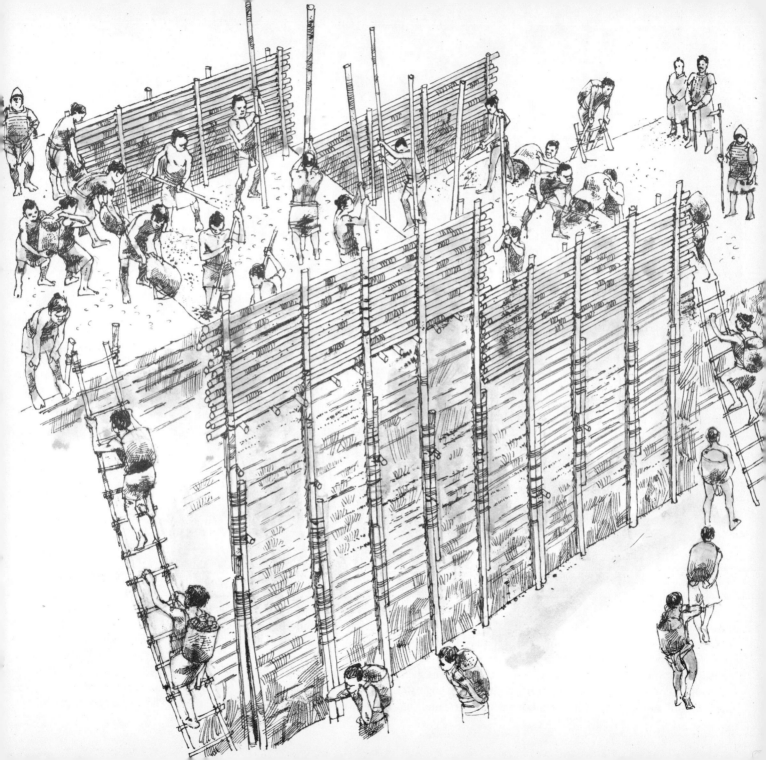

Remains of a frontier wall in the mountains near the borders of present-day Mongolia. This stretch of wall was built during the Ming dynasty (see page 5) and passes through similar country to the Ch'in wall.

The rise of the kingdom of Ch'in

As we can see from the chart on page 30, the kingdom of Ch'in gradually came to control the whole area which had been occupied by the Chinese states. In its conquests of the more powerful of the other states, Ch'in's advance was very rapid indeed. What was it that made Ch'in so successful? One answer is shown by comparing the map opposite with that on page 30.

If you look at the rivers and mountains which surround the area in which the state of Ch'in grew up, you will see that they form a natural fortress, protecting the Ch'in state against attack from the east and south. The most important break in the protection is the Hanku Pass where the Yellow River flows between the mountains. There were also smaller passes in the mountains themselves. These passes have always been key points in the history of China. No matter what state occupied the region, it has always been known as Kuan-nei, the Land Within the Passes. The usefulness of this natural fortress was shown to Ch'in at a very early stage. The states to the east of

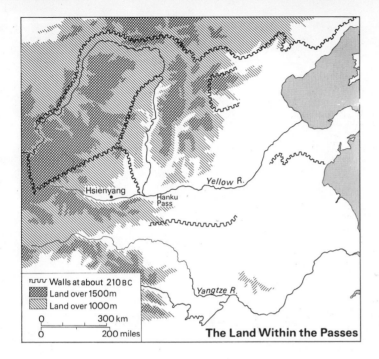

Walls at about 210 BC
Land over 1500 m
Land over 1000 m

0 — 300 km
0 — 200 miles

The Land Within the Passes

Ch'in were afraid that Ch'in was becoming too powerful, and planned to attack the Hanku Pass. However, when the time came, Ch'in was able to concentrate its forces at this one point, and beat off a much bigger army. Ssu-ma Ch'ien's history tells us about this event:

'The noblemen of the other states were afraid of Ch'in, and so they met to discuss how Ch'in could be weakened. With lavish gifts of precious vessels, treasure and rich lands, they bribed the warriors of China to form a united front.

'Their combined army of a million men was drawn from an area ten times bigger than Ch'in, but when they attacked the Pass, the men of Ch'in opened the gates and charged out at them. At this the commanders of the combined army turned tail and ran, not daring to advance, so the noblemen were put to confusion even though Ch'in had not fired a single arrow or thrown a single javelin.'

Although there was probably more fighting than this story tells us, it is still clear that the pass was very difficult to attack. Even when Ch'in had taken over a whole empire, the capital city Hsienyang was kept in the Land Within the Passes.

The people of the state of Ch'in seem to have come originally from the nomad tribes to the west of China and, although they had adopted many Chinese customs, the other Chinese people still thought them rather foreign. The Ch'in people were much tougher than the Chinese themselves. Their methods of fighting were more like those of their nomad ancestors. They used archers on horseback, and guerrilla raids, unlike the Chinese, who still used chariots and foot-soldiers.

The Lord Shang

In about 350 BC, an immigrant came from Wei to Ch'in. His name was Shang Yang, and his arrival in Ch'in must be counted as one of the most important in the chain of events which led to Ch'in's conquest of the rest of China. Shang Yang was one of the Legalist school of philosophy, and he had no time for Mencius' ideas of human goodness (see page 28).

Shang Yang had a different idea. To him, all men seemed naturally bad. He concluded from this that the job of a ruler was quite simply to keep the people under control and prevent them from overthrowing the government. Shang Yang proposed that this should be done by having very strict laws, and imposing them so harshly that the people would be afraid to disobey. The laws which Shang Yang set up would be aimed solely at enriching the state and strengthening the position of the ruler. Once again, Ssu-ma Ch'ien tells us about Shang Yang:

'When Duke Hsiao was on the throne in Ch'in, and planned the expansion of Ch'in, he was assisted by Lord Shang. Shang's domestic policy was to set up laws and measures, to promote ploughing and weaving, and to organise preparation for war. His foreign policy was to make alliance with states to the east of Ch'in in order to attack the more powerful local rulers.'

Work on the land

These drawings, made about 2000 years ago, show people at work on different tasks. Right: *Ploughing and harrowing the fields.*

As we can see from this, Shang Yang was given the title of Lord Shang, and became an adviser to the ruler of Ch'in. Once his ideas had been put into practice, Ch'in rapidly became a very powerful state, self-sufficient in agriculture and weaving, and with a prepared army. All unproductive work, like that of teaching, or trading, was suppressed, and the teachers, traders and others were set to work in productive jobs, to enrich the state. As well as the policies mentioned by Ssu-ma Ch'ien, we also know of others. For example, in order to break the strength of the powerful families of Ch'in, Shang Yang replaced the old local lords by government officials. In the army he introduced a system in which promotion depended only on military skill, which was judged by the number of enemy heads taken in battle.

36

As you may imagine, Shang Yang was creating a ruthless state machine, far removed from the gentlemanly Confucian courts of the other states. This, together with the half-barbarian nature of the people of Ch'in, and the natural defences which surrounded their state, gave them the force which was to lead them to conquer the whole of China. This was achieved in the ruthless way which you would expect. As well as using military force against their victims, the Ch'in leaders used bribery and assassination to weaken the states which they planned to take over. The other states were no match for them. Gradually, Ch'in was moving towards the setting up of a single Chinese empire.

5 The Ch'in empire

In 221 BC when the state of Ch'in had extended its control over all the other Chinese states, the ruler of Ch'in, Prince Cheng, declared himself First Supreme Emperor of Ch'in, which in Chinese is Ch'in Shih Huang-ti.

After Ch'in Shih Huang-ti's unification of the Chinese empire, the laws which had been established in the state of Ch'in under Shang Yang were extended to the whole country by Li Ssu, who was the Emperor's closest adviser. Unification was accompanied by standardisation, and not only were the sizes of weights and measures and the coinage dictated by the government, but so was the style of handwriting, and it was laid down that the official colour for clothing should be black. Even the length of the axles of carts was fixed by law at six ch'ih which is about five feet and three inches (160 cm). This meant that along the rough tracks in remote areas, each cart could follow easily in the ruts left by earlier ones.

As well as standardising the laws and regulations of the empire, Ch'in Shih Huang-ti embarked upon a series of projects designed to preserve the unity of the empire. Many major roads were constructed, canals were dug, and, as Ssu-ma Ch'ien has already told us (on page 7), Meng T'ien, commander of the Ch'in armies, was sent north to construct the Great Wall.

A measuring bowl. The inscription reads: 'As soon as his title was proclaimed the emperor issued a decree to his ministers for regulating differences in laws and in weights and measures. Where doubt existed he established a clear single standard. In the twenty-sixth year of his reign the empire is united and the feudal princes and the black-haired people enjoy peace.' The bowl is made of pottery and would hold about 5 pints (2·5 litres).

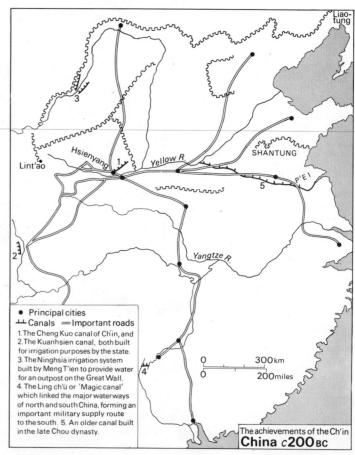

● Principal cities
⊥⊥ Canals ═ Important roads
1. The Cheng Kuo canal of Ch'in, and
2. The Kuanhsien canal, both built for irrigation purposes by the state.
3. The Ninghsia irrigation system built by Meng T'ien to provide water for an outpost on the Great Wall.
4. The Ling ch'ü or 'Magic canal' which linked the major waterways of north and south China, forming an important military supply route to the south. 5. An older canal built in the late Chou dynasty.

The achievements of the Ch'in
China *c* **200** BC

Signalling from a tower on the Ch'in wall, as imagined by a modern artist. One man reports the number and movements of the strangers in the distance. Two men prepare to send smoke signals. A fourth watches for signals from the next tower.

The Great Wall of China

We must not be misled by Ssu-ma Ch'ien's words into thinking that the building of this enormous wall was one single engineering feat. In fact, as we have seen, there were long stretches of wall already in existence along the northern border of China. These Meng T'ien repaired or reconstructed, but he also linked them up with five hundred miles of new wall. This provided the Ch'in empire with a continuous defensive barrier which stretched from Liaotung on the coast near Korea, westwards to the northern bend of the Yellow River, and on to the south to Lint'ao to close off the north-west of the empire from attack.

Ssu-ma Ch'ien tells us that the wall was so effective that the barbarians did not dare to come south with their horses or to bend their bows against Ch'in. In fact, as we have seen, Ch'in Shih Huang-ti must have known very well how to deal with the nomadic barbarians on his northern frontier. The important thing was to be able to prevent the swift nomad horsemen from making a surprise attack. This would give time for the soldiers of the Ch'in empire to counter the attacks. The Great Wall was designed for just this purpose. It had watch-towers spaced along it, so that attacks could be spotted, and signals sent from one tower to the next to call up reinforcements.

This drawing of a hunter, made about 2000 years ago, shows vividly the speed of the nomad archers.

Even though the Great Wall protected the Ch'in empire against attack from outside, its building was a cause of discontent within the empire. As well as the soldiers led by Meng T'ien, hundreds of thousands of other men must have been needed to work on the Wall. We do not know very much about the way in which these men were recruited, or how they worked, because no written records have survived. Even the Chinese themselves did not really know very much. From very early times tales and legends grew up to explain how such an enormous task was carried out. Many of these tales and legends tell of Ch'in Shih Huang-ti's magic powers in constructing the Wall by supernatural means, although others more realistically refer to the hardship and cruelty inflicted on the men who worked on the Wall.

Ch'in Shih Huang-ti was an active emperor, personally involved with much of the day-to-day running of the empire. His regime established an imperial pattern of government which was to form the basis of the Chinese state for over two thousand years. He also built up a continuous line of defence against attack from the north. However, his government oppressed the people to a point where rebellion was never far off. Only his personal grasp on the Legalist political system which had brought him to power kept him firmly established.

right: *The conspiracy of Ch'en She.*

The collapse of the Ch'in empire

When Ch'in Shih Huang-ti died in 210 BC on a visit to the coast of Shantung, the greed for power of his Chief Minister, Li Ssu, and the influential Chief Palace Eunuch, Chao Kao, led to a situation which resulted in the collapse of Ch'in power in a matter of months.

Li Ssu and Chao Kao kept the emperor's death a secret, and transported his body back to the capital under a cartload of dried fish. Once back in the capital, they compelled both the Heir to the Throne and the famous general Meng T'ien to commit suicide. Only then did they announce the emperor's death, and put a young son of Ch'in Shih Huang-ti on the throne as Erh-shih Huang-ti, 'Second Supreme Emperor'. Each aimed to rule the country himself, with Erh-shih Huang-ti as a puppet, but soon Chao Kao had Li Ssu murdered and disposed of Erh-shih Huang-ti in the same way. He then tried to establish one of Erh-shih Huang-ti's sons, Tzu Ying, as king of Ch'in, rather than emperor, but Tzu Ying suspected Chao Kao, and killed him.

The last journey of Ch'in Shih Huang-ti.

In this way, all the main leaders of the empire were killed, and in fact once Ch'in Shih Huang-ti's personal control had gone, the strength of Ch'in began to fade.

The series of revolts which culminated in the final downfall of Ch'in was sparked off in the summer of 209 BC, the first year of the reign of Erh-shih Huang-ti. A labourer of the town of Yangcheng, called Ch'en She was called up with a group of men to serve as soldiers near the Great Wall in the north-east of the empire. Ch'en She was one of the leaders of the group, but he in turn was under the command of three government officers. On the way, the group encountered heavy rains which delayed them badly. One of the laws of Ch'in was that soldiers who did not reach their posts on time would be executed. Ch'en She argued with his fellow soldiers that they might as well kill the government officers and raise a revolt against the Ch'in empire, since if they trudged on to their destination they would in any case be killed. This plan was accepted, and the officers were killed. Shortly afterwards, Ch'en She was proclaimed King of Ch'u. He and the army which he gathered around him set about liberating the land which had been the old state of Ch'u from the domination of the Ch'in emperor (see the map on page 30).

Although Ch'en She died before Ch'in fell, the period of revolt continued after his death. Finally the struggle for control of China resolved itself into a conflict between two men, Hsiang Yü of Ch'u and Liu Pang, one of his former generals.

Hsiang Yü joined Ch'en She's rebellion after only two months, and raised an army to fight for Ch'u against Ch'in. Liu Pang had started a rebellion in the district of P'ei. After the assassination of the local magistrate at the beginning of the rebellion, he was made governor of P'ei. After Ch'en She's death, Hsiang Yü and Liu Pang joined forces against the Ch'in empire. During the conflict they agreed that whoever entered the Land Within the Passes first, and took the Ch'in capital city at Hsienyang, would become the ruler of the empire.

Eventually Liu Pang captured Hsienyang, and the armies of Hsiang Yü defeated the remains of the Ch'in troops in 206 BC. However, despite their previous agreement, a struggle broke out between Liu Pang and Hsiang Yü for control of the empire. By 202 BC, Hsiang Yü's army was on the point of defeat and surrounded by the army of Liu Pang, now king of Han. Hsiang Yü broke out at night with eight hundred horsemen, but the next day the Han army chased them and again surrounded them, several thousand strong. By this time most of Hsiang Yü's men had been lost or killed. Only a few dozen remained with him.

Ssu-ma Ch'ien describes the final scene of the battle for us:

'Hsiang Yü said to his riders, "I will go and catch that general for you!" He commanded them to gallop down in all directions and meet at three places east of the hill. Then he rode down with a great shout, and as the Han army scattered, he beheaded a Han general.

'Hsiang then met his riders at the three appointed places. The Han army did not know where Hsiang had got to, but they split into three groups and again surrounded him. Hsiang then galloped out again, beheading another Han officer and killing eighty or ninety men. When he re-gathered his riders, only two had been lost. Then he said, "What did I say to you?" They all knelt and replied, "It is just as you said."

'Later he commanded his men to dismount and proceed on foot using their short swords in hand to hand fighting. Hsiang himself killed more than a hundred Han soldiers, receiving at least a dozen wounds. He turned his head and seeing an official of the Han army, Lü Ma-t'ung, he said, "Were you not one of my men?" Ma-t'ung faced him and pointed him out, saying, "That is Hsiang!" Then Hsiang said, "I hear that Han has put a reward of a thousand pieces of gold and a fief of ten thousand households on my head. I am going to do you a great favour." With that he cut his own throat and died.'

In the scuffle which followed, his body was hacked into five pieces, five men each taking a piece. When the pieces were later laid out, and the body identified, each man received one-fifth of the reward.

So in 202 BC ended the last resistance to the reign of Liu Pang, first emperor of the *Han* dynasty.

The death of Hsiang Yü.

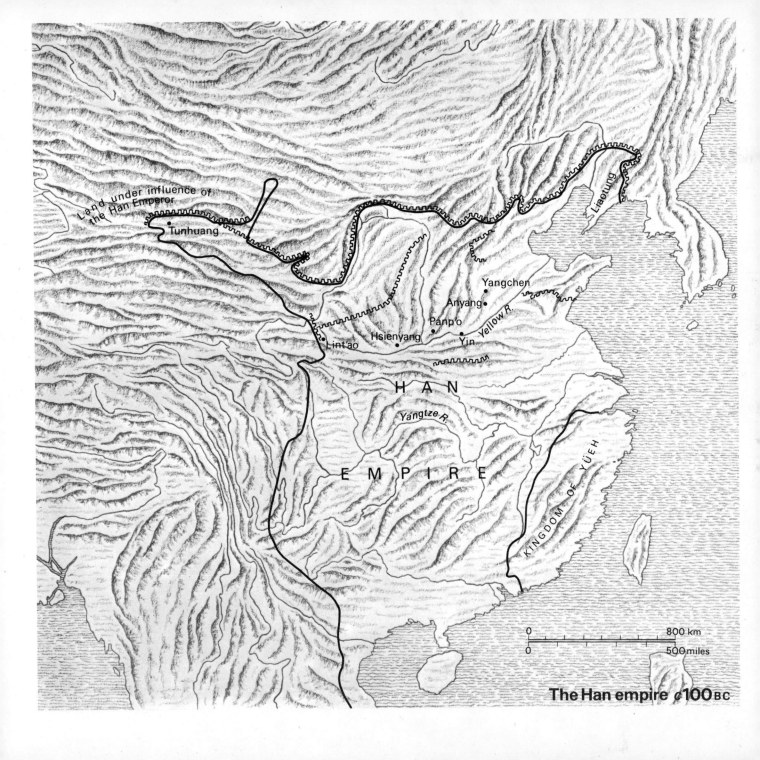

Land under influence of
the Han Emperor

Tunhuang

Liaotung

Yangchen

Anyang

Panp'o

Hsienyang

Lintao

Yin

Yellow R.

H A N

Yangtze R.

E M P I R E

KINGDOM OF YÜEH

0   800 km
0   500 miles

The Han empire c**100** BC

6 The Han dynasty

Expansion of the empire

After the collapse of Ch'in and the founding of the Han dynasty, the defensive line of the Ch'in wall was not fully manned. The northern region of the Han empire was soon invaded by nomadic peoples from the north. These peoples were called by the Chinese the Hsiung-nu. (They may have been the same people as the Huns who later migrated across Asia and into Europe to attack the Roman Empire.)

To begin with, the Han emperors tried to make treaties with the Hsiung-nu. Later, as their empire became stronger, they could wage war or use diplomatic negotiations among the small kingdoms of central Asia. They wanted both to prevent the enemy from invading China, and to protect the trade route which was growing up between China and the West. In the course of this activity, much of which took place in the reign of the Emperor Wu-ti (141–87 BC), the area controlled by the Han empire increased greatly to the north-west (see the map on page 43). Much of the territory beyond Tunhuang was not ruled directly by the Han emperor, but by means of alliances with small local kingdoms. Nevertheless, the aim was to provide a 'corridor', safe from Hsiung-nu attack, for the trade caravans which passed between China and the central Asian states. These states acted as middle-men in the transport of silk from China to the Mediterranean world.

More wall-building

The land as far westward as Tunhuang was gradually brought under the control of the Han empire between about 104 BC and 67 BC. A westward extension of the Great Wall was built to provide a defensive line against attack from the north. The whole of the extended northern frontier of the empire was thus marked by a wall. We can tell from the remains which still survive in the Tunhuang region that there was probably a complex system of watch-towers and garrisons set out along the

above: *Remains of a watch-tower on the wall near Tunhuang.*

below: *Remains of the border wall, built of layers of reed bundles and clay, in the desert near Tunhuang.*

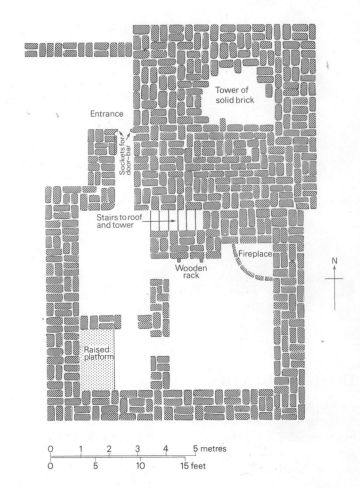

left: A Han watch-tower, still standing today. You can see the core of pounded earth and the remains of the brickwork facings. The plan below shows how living accommodation for a small garrison was built on the Chinese side of the solid tower.

Tower of solid brick

Entrance

Sockets for door-bar

Stairs to roof and tower

Fireplace

Wooden rack

N

Raised platform

0 1 2 3 4 5 metres

0   5   10   15 feet

wall to provide for its defence from Liaotung in the east to Tunhuang in the west. From these remains we can tell more about the construction of the wall.

Pounded earth was still used as the basic building material. You can see from the picture how the desert winds have eroded gaps in the wall, but its survival for over 2000 years shows the strength of this type of wall. Its strength was increased by placing layers of reeds in the pounded earth. In one place, bundles of reeds have been found, neatly laid out at intervals on the Chinese side of the line. These were probably put there in readiness for repairs.

Some of the Han watch-towers have survived better. We can see how at this time the earth core was often faced with baked clay bricks. Other forts and towers were built mainly of brick, and excavations have shown what the plan of a typical watch-tower would have been.

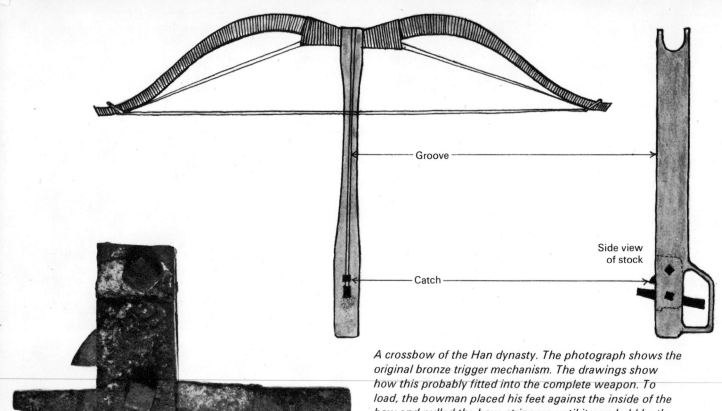

Groove

Catch

Side view
of stock

*A crossbow of the Han dynasty. The photograph shows the
original bronze trigger mechanism. The drawings show
how this probably fitted into the complete weapon. To
load, the bowman placed his feet against the inside of the
bow and pulled the bow-string up until it was held by the
catch. The bolt was then fitted into the groove on top of the
stock. When the trigger was pulled the catch was released
and the missile discharged. The trigger mechanism is
7·5 inches (18 cm) across.*

The Han wall and the men who guarded it

As well as knowing how the Han wall, its towers and forts were
built, we also know more about how the wall was manned.
Many remains of the Han garrisons have been found. There are
shoes and fragments of clothing, bowls and weapons, even
objects like cross-bow triggers. Many 'documents' still survive.
These documents were not written on paper, but on wooden
tablets or slips of bamboo. They consist of various lists,
accounts, registers, records and reports. Some of the slips were
found to be laced together in book form, like the example
shown opposite, which records the granting of leave to a man
called Cheng She when his father died in 42 BC.

We know from these documents that a watch-tower would
have been equipped with cross-bows, bolts or arrows, arrowheads and javelins, with tools, signalling flags, torches and
flares, and with many other purely domestic items like cooking
pots, medicine chests, and a kennel for the garrison dogs.

One of the principal weapons was the crossbow. We know
from a number of labels that they were made in different
strengths. The commanding officers of the soldiers were tested
in archery. A report survives of the test of Wang Wu-ho, in
accordance with the Proficiency Ordinance, in the autumn of
57 BC. Wang shot twelve arrows in his test, and as six of them hit
the target, he passed. Six was the minimum pass mark, and each
extra hit obtained a reward for the marksman.

In the desert regions a slope of sand was made outside the

wall. Each morning patrols, possibly with dogs, went out to check the sand for the tracks of any intruders. Each patrol reported on its findings and these reports were filed. Even the Chinese were not supposed to cross the sand.

Detailed regulations listed the signals to be used when the enemy was sighted. Flags, beacons and smoke signals were to be used, in a code which told what form of attack was in progress.

Military units could keep in touch with each other by means of a regular postal service, and labels from letters have been found. The mail was taken on horseback or by a runner, and scheduled times were set for given journeys.

The wall also served to control the movements of civilians into and out of China. Passports were issued, and records of applicants kept.

All this shows an efficient military system at work, and leaves no doubt that the task of guarding the northern frontier of China was a serious one. Although through the centuries following the Han period, the wall was not always regarded with the same importance, and its line was changed, it was to form the northern frontier of China for more than fifteen hundred years. The wall came to symbolise the isolation of China from the rest of the world.

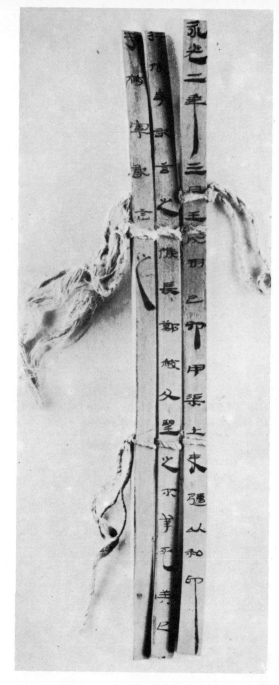

Cheng She's leave pass. 'Books' laced together like this gave rise to the Chinese custom of writing in vertical columns rather than on horizontal lines.

Guide to Pronunciation of Chinese Names

The pronunciations given here indicate the approximate sound of some of the names in this book. The letters *ow* should be pronounced as in the English word *how; eh* represents the vowel sound in *the; g* is always hard.

Chao	*Jow*	Liaotung	*Liow·doong*
Chao Kao	*Jow Gow*	Ling chiu	*Ling chiew*
Ch'en She	*Chehn Sheh*	Lint'ao	*Lin·tow*
Cheng She	*Jehng Sheh*	Li Ssu	*Lee Sseh*
Cheng	*Jehng*	Liu Pang	*Liew Bang*
Cheng Kuo	*Jehng Gwo*	Lu	*Loo*
Ch'i	*Chee*	Lü Ma-t'ung	*Liew Ma-toong*
Chieh	*Jye*		
ch'ih	*chur*	Mencius	*Men·shus*
Chin	*Chin*	Meng T'ien	*Mehng Tien*
Ch'in Shih Huang-ti	*Chin Shur Hwong-dee*		
Chou	*Joh*	Ninghsia	*Ning·sseah*
Ch'u	*Choo*		
		Panp'o	*Ban·paw*
Erh-shih Huang-ti	*Er-shur Hwong-dee*	P'ei	*Pay*
Hanku Pass	*Han·goo*	Shang-ti	*Shang-dee*
Hsia	*Sseah*	Shou	*Show*
Hsiang Yü	*Sseang Yiew*	Ssu-ma Ch'ien	*Sseh-ma Chien*
Hsiao	*Ssiow*		
Hsienyang	*Ssien·yang*	T'ai Shan	*Tie Shan*
Hsiung-nu	*Ssyoong-noo*	T'ang	*Tang*
Hsün-tzu	*Ssyoon-dz*	Ti	*Dee*
		Tunhuang	*Doon·hwong*
Jung	*Roong*	Tzu Ying	*Dz Ying*
ko	*geh*	Wang Wu-ho	*Wong Woo-heh*
Kong-wu Hsiung	*Goong-woo Ssyoong*	Wei	*Way*
Kuanhsien	*Gwan·ssien*	Wu-ti	*Woo-dee*
Kuan-nei	*Gwan-neigh*	Wu Ting	*Woo Ding*
		Yangcheng	*Yang·chehng*

Index

agriculture, origins of, 8, 10
ancestor worship, 14, 15, 20, 26
Anyang, 16, 22
astronomy in Shang period, 15

bone inscriptions from Shang period, 14-15
Book of Documents, 22, 24
bronze: making of, 13-14, 26; moulds for, 18; vessels, ceremonial, 18-19, 20, 23, 24; weapons, 14, 27
Bronze Age, 14

calendar in Shang period, 15
Chao, 31, 32
Chao Kao, 40
Cheng. *See* Ch'in Shi Huang-ti
Cheng She, 46, 47
Ch'en She, 41
Ch'i, 31
Chieh, King, 15
Chin, 31
Ch'in dynasty, 7, 32, 38, 39, 44; collapse of, 38; empire of, 38; expansion of, 31, 34-37
Ch'in Shih Huang-ti, 38, 39, 40, 41
Chou dynasty, 7, 22, 23-25, 26, 27
Ch'u, 31, 41
cities, development of, 16, 26
Confucian philosophy, 27-28, 37
Confucius, 27, 28, 37
crafts, development of, 14, 16
crossbow, Han, 46

dynasty, definition of, 7

Erh-shih Huang-ti, 40, 41

fiefs during Chou period, 23, 24-25
fortune-tellers in Shang period, 15, 19, 20

Hadrian's Wall (Britain), 5
Han dynasty, 7, 31, 45-47; expansion of, 44; founding of, 41-42
Hanku Pass, 34, 35
Historical Annals, 7
Hsia dynasty, 13, 14, 15
Hsiang Yü, 41-42
Hsiao, Duke, 35
Hsienyang, 35, 41
Hsiung-nu, 44
Hsün-tzu, 28
human sacrifice in Shang period, 16

iron, 27; cast, 28

jade carving, 16
Jung, 7, 8, 32

ko (weapon), 18
Kong-wu Hsiung, 23
Kuanhsien, 48
Kuan-nei (Land Within the Passes), 34, 35, 41

Land Within the Passes (Kuan-nei), 34, 35, 41

Legalism (school of philosophy), 28, 35
legends of prehistoric times, 8, 9, 14
Liaotung, 7, 39, 45
Lint'ao, 7, 39
Li Ssu, 38, 40
Liu Pang, 41-42
lost-wax method of casting, 18-19
Lu, 25, 27, 31
Lü Ma-t'ung, 42

Mencius, 27-28, 35
Meng T'ien, 7, 38, 39, 40
Ming dynasty, 5
Mongolia, 34

Neolithic period, 11, 14

'oracle bones', 15

Panp'o, 10
P'ei, 41
Peking, 5, 9
Peking Man, 9
porcelain, 20
potter's wheel, 20
pottery, 20, 26, 28; in Shang period, 16, 20
prehistoric period, 9-14

religion, 14, 18, 20, 24, 26
Rites, The (Chou period), 25

Shang dynasty, 7, 20, 23, 24, 26, 27;
    bronze crafts of, 18-19; cities of, 16;
    fall of, 22; kings of, 14, 15-16, 22;
    origins of, 14, 15-16; tombs of, 16, 18
Shang-ti, 15
Shang Yang, 35-37, 38
Shensi (province), 10
Shensi Mountains, 8
Shou, King, 22
silk trade with the West, 44
Spring and Autumn Annals, The, 25
Spring and Autumn period (Chou
    dynasty), 25, 26, 27
Ssu-ma Ch'ien, 9, 13, 20, 23; and
    description of Ch'in period, 35, 36,
    42; and description of Great Wall,
    7-8, 38, 39; and description of
    Shang dynasty, 14, 15-16, 22

T'ai Shan mountains, 31
T'ang, Duke, 15, 20, 21
Ti, 7, 8, 32
tombs, Shang, 16, 18
towns, development of, 14
Tunhuang, 44, 45
Tzu Ying, 40, 41

walls: city, 16, 32; construction of, 12,
    32, 45; frontier, 28, 31-32, 38-40,
    44-47; 'inner', 31, 32; perimeter,
    11-12, 26; watchtowers on, 45, 46-47
Wang Wu-ho, 46
warfare, 16, 18, 25, 28, 36, 41-42
Warring States, Period of the, 28, 30,
    32
watchtowers, Han, 45-47
weapons, 14, 18, 28, 46
Wei, 31, 32, 35
writing, development of, 14, 21, 27
Wu, King, 22
Wu-ti, Emperor, 44
Wu Ting, 20, 21

vessels, ceremonial, 18-19, 20, 23, 24
villages, early, 10; defences of, 11-12

Yangcheng, 41
Yangtse (river), 32
Yellow River, 7, 34, 39
Yen, 32
Yin (city), 16
Yin (region), 20, 21

Acknowledgments

The author and publisher would like to thank the following for permission to reproduce illustrations:
p.6 Camera and Pen International; pp.8, 34 Camera Press; pp.10 (Excavation), 12 (drawing), 26 from Joseph Needham: *Science and Civilisation in China*, vol 4, part 3, Cambridge University Press; pp.10 (amphora and bowl), 18, 19, 23, 24, 25, 27 (Confucius) and 46 the Trustees of the British Museum; pp.15, 31, 36, 37 and 40 Wen Wu Press, Peking; pp.16, 20, 28 (iron mould), 38 Robert Harding Associates and Times Newspapers Limited; p.22 Imperial Palace Museum, Peking; p.27 (Mencius) Cambridge University Library; pp.44, 45 from M. A. Stein, *Ruins of Desert Cathay* (1913); Allen & Unwin Limited for the extract from A. Waley: *Book of Odes* on p.20.

Cover and text drawings by Mark Peppé
Maps and diagrams by Reg Piggott

Above: *A Han official and his retinue. A rubbing of a tomb tile.*

The Cambridge History Library

The Cambridge Introduction to History
Written by Trevor Cairns

PEOPLE BECOME CIVILIZED

THE ROMANS AND THEIR EMPIRE

BARBARIANS, CHRISTIANS, AND MUSLIMS

THE MIDDLE AGES

EUROPE AROUND THE WORLD

EUROPE AND THE WORLD

THE BIRTH OF MODERN EUROPE

THE OLD REGIME AND THE REVOLUTION

POWER FOR THE PEOPLE

The Cambridge Topic Books
General Editor Trevor Cairns

THE AMERICAN WAR OF INDEPENDENCE

BENIN: AN AFRICAN KINDGOM AND CULTURE

THE BUDDHA

BUILDING THE MEDIEVAL CATHEDRALS

CHRISTOPHER WREN
AND ST. PAUL'S CATHEDRAL

THE EARLIEST FARMERS AND THE FIRST CITIES

EARLY CHINA AND THE WALL

THE FIRST SHIPS AROUND THE WORLD

GANDHI AND THE STRUGGLE
FOR INDIA'S INDEPENDENCE

HERNAN CORTES: CONQUISTADOR IN MEXICO

THE INDUSTRIAL REVOLUTION BEGINS

LIFE IN A FIFTEENTH-CENTURY MONASTERY

LIFE IN A MEDIEVAL VILLAGE

LIFE IN THE IRON AGE

LIFE IN THE OLD STONE AGE

MARTIN LUTHER

MEIJI JAPAN

THE MURDER OF ARCHBISHOP THOMAS

MUSLIM SPAIN

THE NAVY THAT BEAT NAPOLEON

POMPEII

THE PYRAMIDS

THE ROMAN ARMY

THE ROMAN ENGINEERS

ST. PATRICK AND IRISH CHRISTIANITY

THE VIKING SHIPS

The Cambridge History Library will be expanded in the future to include additional volumes. Lerner Publications Company is pleased to participate in making this excellent series of books available to a wide audience of readers.

Lerner Publications Company
241 First Avenue North, Minneapolis, Minnesota 55401